THE PILGRIM PERIOD

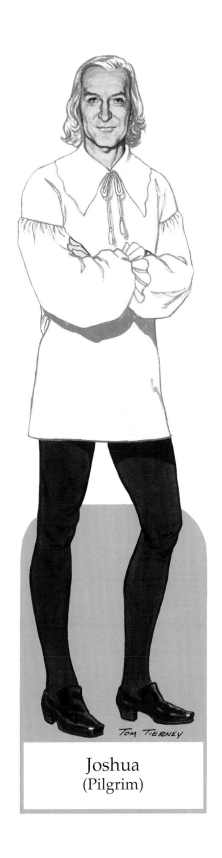

Joshua
(Pilgrim)

Patience
(Pilgrim)

PLATE 1

Patience

Pilgrim
(Plate 1)

Joshua

Pilgrim
(Plate 1)

THE PILGRIM PERIOD

Adam
(Pilgrim)

Marta
(Pilgrim)

PLATE 2

Marta

Pilgrim
(Plate 2)

Adam

Pilgrim
(Plate 2)

The Pilgrim Period

Henry
(Pilgrim)

Samuel & Anne
(Pilgrim)

Amity
(Pilgrim)

Plate 3

Amity

Pilgrim
(Plate 3)

Henry

Pilgrim
(Plate 3)

Samuel & Anne

Pilgrim
(Plate 3)

Benjamin

Colonial
(Plate 4)

Sarah

Colonial
(Plate 4)

Ruth
& Thomas

Colonial
(Plate 4)

THE COLONIAL PERIOD

Sarah
(Colonial)

Ruth
& Thomas
(Colonial)

Benjamin
(Colonial)

PLATE 4

THE COLONIAL PERIOD

John
(Colonial)

Prudence
(Colonial)

PLATE 5

Prudence

Colonial
(Plate 5)

John

Colonial
(Plate 5)

Hannah

Colonial
(Plate 6)

Samuel

Colonial
(Plate 6)

THE COLONIAL PERIOD

Samuel
(Colonial)

Hannah
(Colonial)

PLATE 6

THE FEDERAL PERIOD

Mary Lou
(Federal)

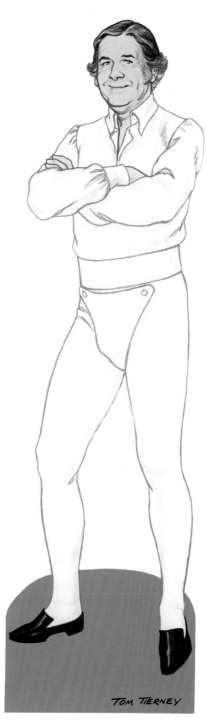

John
(Federal)

PLATE 7

John

Federal
(Plate 7)

Mary Lou

Federal
(Plate 7)

Patricia

Federal
(Plate 8)

Walter

Federal
(Plate 8)

THE FEDERAL PERIOD

Walter
(Federal)

Patricia
(Federal)

PLATE 8

THE FEDERAL PERIOD

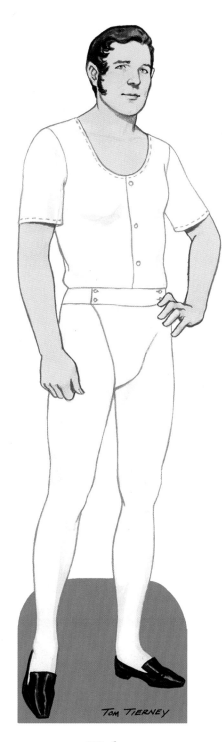

Hal
(Federal)

Stan, Sharon & Tom
(Federal)

Kathy
(Federal)

PLATE 9

Kathy

Federal
(Plate 9)

Stan,
Sharon & Tom

Federal
(Plate 9)

Hal

Federal
(Plate 9)

Ruth

Civil War
(Plate 10)

Gregory

Civil War
(Plate 10)

Gregory
(Civil War)

Ruth
(Civil War)

PLATE 10

THE CIVIL WAR PERIOD

Julia
(Civil War)

Theodore
(Civil War)

PLATE 11

Theodore

Civil War
(Plate 11)

Julia

Civil War
(Plate 11)

Richard, Kenneth
& Annie

Civil War
(Plate 12)

Tom

Civil War
(Plate 12)

Christine

Civil War
(Plate 12)

Richard, Kenneth
& Annie
(Civil War)

Christine
(Civil War)

Tom
(Civil War)

PLATE 12

THE PILGRIM PERIOD

Joshua

Patience

PLATE 13

Patience

Pilgrim
(Plate 13)

Joshua

Pilgrim
(Plate 13)

THE PILGRIM PERIOD

Henry

Samuel & Anne

Amity

PLATE 15

Amity

Pilgrim
(Plate 15)

Henry

Pilgrim
(Plate 15)

Samuel & Anne

Pilgrim
(Plate 15)

Patience

Pilgrim
(Plate 16)

Joshua

Pilgrim
(Plate 16)

THE PILGRIM PERIOD

Joshua

Patience

PLATE 16

THE PILGRIM PERIOD

Adam

Marta

PLATE 17

Marta

Pilgrim
(Plate 17)

Adam

Pilgrim
(Plate 17)

Amity

Pilgrim
(Plate 18)

Henry

Pilgrim
(Plate 18)

Samuel & Anne

Pilgrim
(Plate 18)

THE PILGRIM PERIOD

Do not cut out white areas between arms and body.

Henry

Samuel & Anne

Amity

PLATE 18

THE PILGRIM PERIOD

Joshua

Patience

PLATE 19

Patience

Pilgrim
(Plate 19)

Joshua

Pilgrim
(Plate 19)

Marta

Pilgrim
(Plate 20)

Adam

Pilgrim
(Plate 20)

THE PILGRIM PERIOD

Adam

Marta

PLATE 20

THE PILGRIM PERIOD

cut on dashed line

Henry

Samuel & Anne

Amity

PLATE 21

Amity

Pilgrim
(Plate 21)

Henry

Pilgrim
(Plate 21)

Samuel & Anne

Pilgrim
(Plate 21)

Patience

Pilgrim
(Plate 22)

Joshua

Pilgrim
(Plate 22)

THE PILGRIM PERIOD

Joshua

Patience

PLATE 22

THE PILGRIM PERIOD

Do not cut out white areas between arms and body.

Adam

Marta

PLATE 23

Marta

Pilgrim
(Plate 23)

Adam

Pilgrim
(Plate 23)

Amity

Pilgrim
(Plate 24)

Henry

Pilgrim
(Plate 24)

Samuel & Anne

Pilgrim
(Plate 24)

THE PILGRIM PERIOD

Do not cut out white area between arm and body.

Henry

Samuel & Anne

Amity

PLATE 24

THE COLONIAL PERIOD

SR

BE

cut on dashed line

BE

RT

RT

Sarah

Ruth & Thomas

Benjamin

PLATE 25

BE

Benjamin

Colonial
(Plate 25)

Sarah

Colonial
(Plate 25)

Ruth & Thomas

Colonial
(Plate 25)

JN

John

Colonial
(Plate 26)

Prudence

Colonial
(Plate 26)

The Colonial Period

cut on dashed line →

Prudence

John

Plate 26

THE COLONIAL PERIOD

Samuel

Hannah

PLATE 27

Samuel

Colonial
(Plate 27)

Hannah

Colonial
(Plate 27)

Ruth & Thomas

Colonial
(Plate 28)

Benjamin

Colonial
(Plate 28)

Sarah

Colonial
(Plate 28)

THE COLONIAL PERIOD

BE

cut on dashed line

Do not cut out
white areas
between arms
and body.

BE

RT

RT

RT

SR

SR

RT

Ruth & Thomas

Benjamin

Sarah

PLATE 28

THE COLONIAL PERIOD

cut on dashed line

John

Prudence

PLATE 29

Prudence

Colonial
(Plate 29)

John

Colonial
(Plate 29)

Hannah

Colonial
(Plate 30)

Samuel

Colonial
(Plate 30)

THE COLONIAL PERIOD

Samuel

Hannah

PLATE 30

THE COLONIAL PERIOD

cut on dashed line

Benjamin

Ruth & Thomas

Sarah

PLATE 31

Sarah

Colonial
(Plate 31)

Benjamin

Colonial
(Plate 31)

Ruth & Thomas

Colonial
(Plate 31)

John

Colonial
(Plate 32)

Prudence

Colonial
(Plate 32)

THE COLONIAL PERIOD

John

Prudence

PLATE 32

THE COLONIAL PERIOD

Samuel

Hannah

PLATE 33

Samuel

Colonial
(Plate 33)

Hannah

Colonial
(Plate 33)

Benjamin

Colonial
(Plate 34)

Sarah

Colonial
(Plate 34)

Ruth & Thomas

Colonial
(Plate 34)

THE COLONIAL PERIOD

cut on dashed line

Sarah

Benjamin

Ruth & Thomas

PLATE 34

THE COLONIAL PERIOD

Prudence

John

PLATE 35

Prudence

Colonial
(Plate 35)

John

Colonial
(Plate 35)

Samuel

Colonial
(Plate 36)

Hannah

Colonial
(Plate 36)

THE COLONIAL PERIOD

Samuel

Hannah

PLATE 36

THE FEDERAL PERIOD

Mary Lou

cut on dashed line

John

PLATE 37

JN

John

Federal
(Plate 37)

Mary Lou

Federal
(Plate 37)

Patricia

Federal
(Plate 38)

Walter

Federal
(Plate 38)

THE FEDERAL PERIOD

cut on dashed line

Walter

Patricia

PLATE 38

THE FEDERAL PERIOD

HL

cut on dashed line

HL

KA

cut on
dashed line

SST

Hal

Stan, Sharon & Tom

Kathy

PLATE 39

HL

SST

Kathy

Federal
(Plate 39)

Hal

Federal
(Plate 39)

Stan, Sharon
& Tom

Federal
(Plate 39)

JN

John

Federal
(Plate 40)

Mary Lou

Federal
(Plate 40)

THE FEDERAL PERIOD

cut on dashed line

Mary Lou

John

PLATE 40

THE FEDERAL PERIOD

Walter

Patricia

PLATE 41

Patricia

Federal
(Plate 41)

Walter

Federal
(Plate 41)

HL

Kathy

Federal
(Plate 42)

Stan, Sharon
& Tom

Federal
(Plate 42)

Hal

Federal
(Plate 42)

Federal
(Plate 42)

THE FEDERAL PERIOD

cut on dashed line

HL

KA

SST

SST

do not cut out white area
between arm and body

Hal

Stan, Sharon & Tom

Kathy

PLATE 42

THE FEDERAL PERIOD

Mary Lou

John

PLATE 43

John

Federal
(Plate 43)

Mary Lou

Federal
(Plate 43)

WA

Patricia

Federal
(Plate 44)

Walter

Federal
(Plate 44)

THE FEDERAL PERIOD

← cut on dashed line

WA

Walter

PT

PT

Patricia

PLATE 44

THE FEDERAL PERIOD

HL

cut on dashed line

HL

KA

SST

SST

Hal

Stan, Sharon & Tom

Kathy

PLATE 45

Kathy

Federal
(Plate 45)

Hal

Federal
(Plate 45)

Stan, Sharon
& Tom

Federal
(Plate 45)

JN

John

Federal
(Plate 46)

Mary Lou

Federal
(Plate 46)

THE FEDERAL PERIOD

cut on dashed line →

Mary Lou

John

PLATE 46

THE FEDERAL PERIOD

cut on dashed line

WA

PT

Walter

Patricia

PLATE 47

WA

Patricia

Federal
(Plate 47)

Walter

Federal
(Plate 47)

Hal

Federal
(Plate 48)

Brad & Kathy

Federal
(Plate 48)

Stan, Sharon
& Tom

Federal
(Plate 48)

THE FEDERAL PERIOD

Hal

Stan, Sharon & Tom

Brad & Kathy

PLATE 48

THE CIVIL WAR PERIOD

Gregory

Ruth

PLATE 49

Ruth

Civil War
(Plate 49)

Gregory

Civil War
(Plate 49)

TH

Theodore

Civil War
(Plate 50)

Julia

Civil War
(Plate 50)

THE CIVIL WAR PERIOD

cut on solid line →

Julia

Theodore

PLATE 50

THE CIVIL WAR PERIOD

RKA

CH

CH

TO

cut on
solid line

TO

RKA

Richard, Kenneth
& Annie

Christine

Tom

PLATE 51

TO

Richard, Kenneth
& Annie

Civil War
(Plate 51)

Tom

Civil War
(Plate 51)

Christine

Civil War
(Plate 51)

GR

Ruth

Civil War
(Plate 52)

Gregory

Civil War
(Plate 52)

THE CIVIL WAR PERIOD

cut on
solid line

Gregory

Ruth

PLATE 52

THE CIVIL WAR PERIOD

Julia

Theodore

PLATE 53

Theodore

Civil War
(Plate 53)

Julia

Civil War
(Plate 53)

RKA

Richard, Kenneth
& Annie

Civil War
(Plate 54)

Tom

Civil War
(Plate 54)

Christine

Civil War
(Plate 54)

THE CIVIL WAR PERIOD

Christine

Richard, Kenneth
& Annie

Tom

PLATE 54

THE CIVIL WAR PERIOD

Gregory

Ruth

PLATE 55

Ruth

Civil War
(Plate 55)

Gregory

Civil War
(Plate 55)

Theodore

Civil War
(Plate 56)

Julia

Civil War
(Plate 56)

THE CIVIL WAR PERIOD

Julia

Theodore

PLATE 56

THE CIVIL WAR PERIOD

Christine

Richard, Kenneth
& Annie

Tom

PLATE 57

Richard, Kenneth
& Annie

Civil War
(Plate 57)

Tom

Civil War
(Plate 57)

Christine

Civil War
(Plate 57)

GR

Ruth

Civil War
(Plate 58)

Gregory

Civil War
(Plate 58)

THE CIVIL WAR PERIOD

cut on
solid line

Gregory

Ruth

PLATE 58

THE CIVIL WAR PERIOD

cut on
solid line

Julia

Theodore

PLATE 59

TH

Theodore

Civil War
(Plate 59)

Julia

Civil War
(Plate 59)

Richard, Kenneth
& Annie

Civil War
(Plate 60)

Christine & Tom

Civil War
(Plate 60)

THE CIVIL WAR PERIOD

Richard, Kenneth
& Annie

Christine & Tom

PLATE 60

CLOTHING OF THE PILGRIM PERIOD

(NOTE: The dolls are on Plates 1 to 3; Their costumes are on Plates 13 to 24)

In the pioneering days of seventeenth-century America, no two families would have dressed exactly alike. There were no fashion magazines and no patterns to work from. Women, working alone, made their families' clothing by hand. Individual skills and personal preferences varied, leading to numerous variations in style. Overall, however, constraint rather than freedom prevailed. The dress style of most early colonists was limited by community beliefs, by the availability of resources, and by the rigors of life in the New World. Most seventeenth-century clothing was, of necessity, practical and lacked the ornamentation of contemporary European dress.

The first set of paper dolls in this book depicts a middle-class American family of the Pilgrim Period around the middle of the seventeenth century. The family is a fictional one, and the author has taken a few liberties with historical events in order to represent more than one influence on the dress of the time—Puritan and Dutch, as well as Pilgrim. The particular Pilgrim-Dutch intermarriage attributed to this family would probably not have occurred so early in our history. Still, the costumes themselves, which are based on those in old prints and paintings, are authentic.

The family of dolls representing the Pilgrim Period is of predominantly Pilgrim background, but has been strongly influenced by the Puritans (who were far more militant and strict in their religious beliefs than the Pilgrims), and the Dutch. Having resided in the Pilgrim settlement of Plymouth, the family is shown just before and after moving to the Dutch farming area on Manhattan Island to begin a new life.

Plate 1. Grandfather Joshua was born in England of parents who became Pilgrims and migrated to Plymouth. He is wearing a soft linen shirt over knitted woolen hose. Short linen underdrawers were generally worn only by the wealthy in this period. His shirt must do triple duty as underwear, outerwear, and nightwear. Grandmother Patience, of Puritan ancestry, moved to Plymouth when she was a girl. She married Joshua at fifteen and they began farming together. She wears a soft linen chemise with a drawstring at the neckline that can be adjusted for warm or cold weather. Puritan women did not wear such extravagances as underdresses, overdresses, or stomachers. They wore several petticoats, perhaps of bright red wool, for warmth. Over her chemise and petticoat, Patience wears a front-laced linen corset. On her head she wears a "cornet," or "Dutch coif," a starched linen cap.

Plate 2. Adam worked with his father, Joshua, on the farm and also became a skilled trader. He married Marta, the daughter of a prosperous director of the Dutch West India Company. He wears a soft linen shirt much like his father's. The large collar was called a "band," and the tie strings "band strings." Ribbons and decoration were frowned upon by the strictest Pilgrims, and generally buttons and buckles were expensive and hard to come by, so band strings were about as much decoration as was usually found on the clothing of Pilgrim men. Adam's stockings are of worsted yarn. Marta wears a tabbed bodice, boned and stiffened, over a Holland linen chemise. Her cap, which has a softer,

fuller crown than that of her mother-in-law, is a forerunner of the "mob cap" of Revolutionary days.

Plate 3. Adam and Marta's older son, Henry, is an adopted child. He wears a cotton shirt and worsted hose. Amity is Adam and Marta's older daughter. She wears a linen shirt and a deep blue bodice, stiffened with stitching, as well as a bright red petticoat. Younger son, Samuel, wears a cotton shirt of the same kind as those of the other males in the family. His hose is short; it is held in place by the ties on his knee breeches. He is whittling a reed whistle for his little sister. Anne, the youngest of the children, is wearing a chemise and a cap of soft linen. Her shoes are of soft rabbit skin.

The first group of Pilgrim costumes (Plates 13–15) shows the family in their Pilgrim garb. They are dressed for travel because they are leaving Plymouth to resettle on Manhattan Island. Marta's father died recently and she has inherited his farmland and his business holdings, necessitating the move to protect her interests.

Plate 13. Joshua wears a typical Pilgrim costume, made of black woolen material. Over the coat he wears a cape with a large squared collar. His breeches are secured just below the knee with a discreet ribbon tie. His sensible shoes are square-toed and low-heeled. He carries a musket for protection on the long journey over both land and water from Plymouth to Manhattan. Patience wears a plain-cut dress with a moderately full skirt. It has a white bibbed front held in place by flattened bows in lieu of buttons. She wears a large woolen cape as protection against the weather. Puritan and Pilgrim women alike disdained fancy hairstyles and pulled their hair back into tight buns.

Plate 14. Adam wears a brown worsted suit much like his father's, with the cape thrown back to reveal the capped-shoulder detail. The shirt collar is of the square-cut variety, a style that was also popular, although it was originally a Puritan style, and the shirt sleeves are folded back over the coat sleeves to form deep cuffs. Adam's felt hat, like most Pilgrim hats (both men's and women's), is black with a band of the same color on its high crown. If a decoration was worn on the hatband, it was usually restricted to a silver buckle centered in the front. Marta is wearing a simply cut dress in deep maroon. The Pilgrims and Puritans by no means wore black only, but they did generally prefer darker, more sedate colors in their clothing. Marta's bodice, on the other hand, is of Dutch origin, and so has a bright yellow panel down the front with a slender matching apron. On her head is the Dutch coif. The coif is worn both indoors and outdoors, but for outdoor wear she tops it with a hat identical to the man's.

Plate 15. Henry is wearing a suit with the sleeves removed (suit sleeves could be unlaced). Amity's deep yellow dress is a hand-me-down from her mother. It is worn with a ruff, a by-then old-fashioned feature of sixteenth-century costume, as well as a long-pointed collar ending in tassels. Below the bodice is a long, narrow apron. Samuel's sleeveless suit is of beige wool. His breeches' tie has come undone—a common problem with tie closures. Anne wears a jacket and skirt with an apron tied at the waist.

Plates 16–18 illustrate everyday farm wear. Generally this was "best" clothing that, through wear, was relegated to work use.

Plate 16. Joshua wears a sleeveless jacket from one old suit and gray breeches from another. His hat is also an old one that has become rather battered through the years. He is wearing leather riding boots with broad tops. He carries a rake and a sickle for cutting fodder for the animals. Patience is wearing an old jacket of maroon woolen material with a skirt to match. All decoration has been removed and carefully saved for future use on some other garment. Her apron has been tucked back up under her bodice, forming a "pocket."

Plate 17. Adam wears a leather jacket made on the order of the regular suit jacket. Just why the front of these jackets was cut so that the belly was left exposed is unknown, unless it was to allow greater ease of movement. Perhaps the straps with buckles dangling at the sides allowed for closure. It is a style of garment found among the German and Dutch peasants of the period. Adam carries a shovel for digging a new well. Marta wears a bodice over her chemise, with her outer petticoat tucked up under it to form an apron and probably also to keep her cool. She carries a leather bucket for gathering herbs from the kitchen garden.

Plate 18. Henry wears a simple work shirt with pantaloons, a style of garment borrowed from the peasants of Europe. He carries a mallet and an adze for squaring up timbers. Amity wears a dark green jacket over a shirt that has been bloused at the waist. Samuel wears a shirt and pantaloons rolled up over the knees. He is barefoot, as most children were when working in the farmyard in mild weather. Both his and Henry's pantaloons are tied at the waist by a length of rope for a belt. Anne wears an old dress and cap of Amity's from Plymouth days. They are in the Pilgrim style.

Plates 19–21 also show everyday clothes, but these are garments generally worn for less strenuous tasks. Again, they were usually garments formerly used for dress-up occasions.

Plate 19. Joshua is dressed in a leather jerkin with tied-on sleeves. His stockings are white, a mode borrowed from the Dutch. He has stuck a turkey feather in his narrow hatband. Patience is dressed to go calling on a sick friend. She is carrying a basket of food and medicinal herbs as a gift. Her dress is of the traditional Pilgrim type with the additional touch of bands of ribbon stitched around the skirt for stiffening.

Plate 20. Adam wears a leather vest and pantaloons rolled up above the knees for wading in the stream while fishing. His hat is of soft leather. Over her yellow-and-brown bodice and sleeves, Marta wears a white linen capelet. Instead of a cornet, she wears a kerchief over her head, also a Dutch style.

Plate 21. Henry and the other young people are going berry picking. Henry wears a dark blue worsted vest over his shirt and breeches. His hat is of straw and he is stockingless. Amity is wearing a shirt with starched, pleated collar and cuffs under her dark blue jacket with red oversleeves and a corset of boiled leather. Her skirt is of coarse brown wool with bands of stitching at the hem. Samuel wears a soft linen shirt and dark gray breeches rolled up to the knee. Anne wears a buttoned shirt and brown skirt with a blue waistband and white linen apron. She is wearing wooden shoes that her grandfather carved for her.

Plates 22–24 find the family celebrating the wedding of Henry and Amity. (Since they are not blood relations, there is no taboo on their marriage.) As a wedding gift, Adam and Marta are giving them a tract of farmland, and the men of the family and friends will aid them in building a house.

Plate 22. Joshua is wearing a black worsted suit cut in the mid-seventeenth-century English manner, but without the ribbons and furbelows. His collar and cuffs are of Dutch lace, as is all the lace trim on the family's wedding garments. At his waist, he wears a colorful satin sash, indicating that he has become an official of the town. His hat has a soft, somewhat conical crown (again the Dutch influence is apparent) and is ornamented with plumes. Patience is wearing a dress copied from dolls she has seen dressed in the Dutch fashions of a year or so earlier (before the era of fashion magazines, dolls, clothed in the most stylish apparel of the day, were sent regularly by ship from Europe). Her corset has a deep "V" front and the overskirt is caught up under it in a formal arrangement. Her cuffs and collar feature openwork and lace trim. She wears a hood over a crown of ruffles on her forehead, in the French manner, and a cape of black satin matching the trim on her gown.

Plate 23. Adam is wearing a suit basically like the earlier Pilgrim suit, but with a longer, more flaring jacket. His lower-crowned, broader-brimmed hat foreshadows eighteenth-century styles of headwear. Marta's gown has a whalebone corset with matching sleeves and overskirt, which is caught up to reveal her white petticoat. Her deep cuffs and collar are of white linen with openwork and lace edging. She wears a matching hood, lined with white. At her throat is a string of glass beads.

Plate 24. The bridegroom, Henry, wears a jacket with slashed sleeves. His shirt has a square-cut collar and deep cuffs, both trimmed with lace. His shirt is bloused at the waist. His cape and breeches are of dark blue wool, and he wears blue stockings. His colored hatband is a temporary adornment for the wedding. The Dutch community did not have the dress restrictions of the Pilgrims, or, especially, the Puritans. As a result, Amity can wear a wedding dress, petticoat, and shift all of silk. Over her head and face she wears a sheer white veil. Samuel wears a jacket cut like Henry's but without the slashed sleeves. His shirt collar is of the traditional square cut. He wears a short cape and matching short breeches over white hose. He is carrying a Bible for the ceremony. Anne is wearing a dress of the same blue woolen material that Samuel's and Henry's jackets are made of. Her collar and petticoat are of white linen and over her head she wears a short hood.

Note: The abbreviations on the clothing tabs indicate for which person (or group) the garment is intended: JO for Joshua, PA for Patience, AD for Adam, MA for Marta, HE for Henry, SA for Samuel and Anne, and AM for Amity.

CLOTHING OF THE COLONIAL PERIOD

(**NOTE:** The dolls are on Plates 4 to 6; Their costumes are on Plates 25 to 36)

The eight paper dolls seen on Plates 4–6 portray an entire Colonial family, and have been dressed in clothes that represent four different situations in which such a family might have been found.

Grandparents Samuel and Hannah are relatively well-to-do; they have acquired some land and money, and live quite comfortably. Parents John and Prudence are a couple dealing with the everyday struggle of raising and feeding their four children—18-year-old Benjamin; 15-year-old Sarah; Ruth, 6 years old; and Thomas, age 2.

Plate 4. Sarah's chemise often doubles as a "lounging" or "morning" dress. Her red shoes of silk brocade are very fashionable for young ladies of this period. Ruth wears a chemise with tucked sleeves and an Empire-type waist—a popular style in children's wear. Her little brother, Thomas, wears a shirt and diapers; because of a shortage of pins during the Revolutionary period, the diapers were tied in place. Benjamin wears drawers of natural linen with stockings and shoes; the opening in the trousers is called a front fall.

Plate 5. Mother Prudence wears a laced corset with panniers (a hooped framework designed to give width to the gowns of this period; the hoops were of cane, whalebone, or wire) over a muslin camisole which also doubles as a nightgown. The corset and shoes are both of embroidered damask. Father John's soft shirt is worn with footed drawers of red flannel. The legs are separate pieces joined at the waistband. The small gathers at the waist and a drawstring at the back give the proper fit.

Plate 6. Grandfather Samuel's bloused top doubles as both shirt and undershirt in addition to being a nightshirt. The drawers are of natural, soft linen; the straight-cut legs are wrapped around and tied at the knee to accommodate knee breeches. Grandmother Hannah demonstrates the fact that there is no clear-cut definition for underwear in the Colonial period—her laced corset is made of the same fabric as her gown (see Plate 33) and has removable sleeves that tie in place. Oval hoops are sewn into a flannel skirt to create panniers.

The first group of Colonial costumes (Plates 25–27) represents traditional working-class clothes made of coarsely woven fabrics, often homespun, and devoid of embroidered buttonholes, ruffles, lace, and other embellishments. The garments generally were drab in color; brown was the most easily obtained dyestuff during this time. Many German immigrants settled in the Hudson Valley, Pennsylvania, the Carolinas, and Virginia, imparting a German influence to the clothes.

Plate 25. Sarah's simple bodice closes with hook fasteners down the front. The sleeves are pleated at the cuffs to curve with the arm. She wears knitted mitts for warmth; they are fingerless to allow for movement. The apron she wears is pinned in place (thus the name "pinafore" developed). Benjamin wears a blue smock with knicker trousers and striped stockings, which were common at this time. He wears a bandanna neckerchief and wide-brimmed felt hat. Ruth wears a simple dress without sleeves. Her chemise sleeves are pushed up to the elbow and she wears a kerchief at her neck and an apron tied about her waist. Thomas wears a coat with an apron. The apron is a square yard of fabric, cut off at the top corners to make a bib. It is attached to his coat button with a buttonhole and is belted with a leather cord.

Plate 26. Prudence is dressed as a farmer's wife in an outfit showing German influence. Her bodice is attached to the corset and decorated with ribbon; the elbow-length sleeves have shaped cuffs. Her gauze apron is for "dress-up" and is held on by a cloth belt. Her red, turned-up shoes are highly prized by rural folk. John's work clothes are of homespun cloth in dark colors; the shirt has a dropped shoulder, a style popular well into the nineteenth century; there is probably a ruffle at the cuff which is worn folded inside for everyday wear. He wears a flat felt hat and carries a powder horn and a shoulder pouch containing shells.

Plate 27. Samuel is wearing a brocade banian over a waistcoat and knee breeches; the waistcoat is open for ventilation. The banian, extremely popular with men of all ages during the 1750s–1770s, is worn at gatherings or in public for dining and drinking occasions. A tam-o'-shanter is worn when Samuel's wig is off (sometimes in winter he wears a fur cap). Hannah's brown linen dress (consisting of corset, sleeves, chemise, and skirt) is layered with a bodiced overskirt of gauze as well as a large kerchief of embroidered and ribboned gauze. Hannah wears a mobcap of sheer white lawn with lace trim and a pink taffeta ribbon. Her fan is Chinese and her fingerless gloves are of brown lace.

The second group of costumes (Plates 28–30) changes the dolls into a middle-class family during the Revolution. Although a few militia companies had uniforms, the chief uniforms during the early years of the war were smocks and hunting clothes; regiments from different areas were distinguished by different colors. Regarding women's clothes, by the time of the Revolution, the sacque or "Watteau" gown (worn by Prudence in Plate 29) was old-fashioned in Europe. However, owing to the cost and scarcity of imported silks and fancy fabrics, American women nursed their dresses into extended service through the end of the Revolution.

Plate 28. Young Benjamin has joined the militia and wears a linen hunting shirt with double fringed collars for extra protection during wet and cold weather. Every seam in the shirt is covered with fringe to prevent water from penetrating the seams. He is wearing regular knee breeches, but his shins are covered by leather leggings held up by beaded and fringed garters. He wears a leather ammunition pack. Sarah is wearing a silk faille bodice with a matching green overskirt pulled up toward the back (a forerunner of the bustle) over a printed cotton petticoat. Her chemise shows at the neck and sleeves. Ruth's cotton dress features shirring on the sleeves and a center panel of shirring on the bodice. Thomas's coat is brown wool with red silk trim. He wears a tan cotton dress over a white shirt and a soft felt hat with a pink plume.

Plate 29. John is wearing an Army officer's uniform in the colors of Virginia—a dark blue coat with red lapels and lining. His hat is notable because it is the new bicorne or two-cornered hat. Prudence is wearing the sacque or "Watteau" gown with a shirred border at the front opening and on the sleeves and turban. The seams in this full gown's waist area could be let out, converting it into a maternity garment quite easily.

Plate 30. During the Revolution, Samuel calls upon his experiences as a young sailor to become a privateer for the new Continental Navy. Although there are no official Navy uniforms, privateer officers dress in the formal uniforms of military officers. Hannah is wearing a linen dress with a divided skirt; the front opening is bordered along each side with crewel-embroidered panels. The bodice is laced over the chemise in a zigzag pattern. The sleeves of the bodice are quite short, revealing fitted chemise sleeves. The petticoat is quilted and decorated with crewel embroidery.

In Plates 31–33, the Colonial family is dressed in the garments worn by the upper-middle class near the end of the Revolution.

Plate 31. Children's clothes closely followed those of the adults during this time. Benjamin's formal coat has the large cuffs characteristic of this period. The coat is different from other styles in that it has a small standup collar. His coat and trousers are of purple ottoman; the vest is mauve with silver brocade. Sarah's dress is of printed linen. The bodice is fitted over a corset in front; fullness in back gives a cape-like appearance. The skirt is shorter than that of an older woman. Ruth wears a yellow silk print dress; her camisole forms a ruffle at the neck and sleeves. Her apron and cap are of soft white linen. Thomas's outfit shows that boys do not wear trousers until they are out of diapers. He wears a coat of brown and oxblood-red velvet. The ribbon around his neck also holds his back curls in place.

Plate 32. Prudence wears a dress of imported silk. The bodice is worn over a matching corset and joins at the center front with concealed hooks; the elbow-length sleeves have a ruffle that is worn turned back. Her hair is "creped" and powdered (to crepe, the hair was tightly curled with an iron, then teased out until it stood quite high); the back of her hair is worn in large spiral curls. She wears a small cap, or fontange, of ecru and white lace. John's formal suit is of blue satin with silver trim buttons. The waistcoat is of a pale blue silk taffeta with elaborate ribbon and silver-embroidered trim. His shoes have a modified tongue treatment, but he wears the ubiquitous silver buckles that are a status symbol.

Plate 33. Samuel's formal suit is of green velvet with silver braid and silver buttons. The large pocket flaps, quite in vogue, are worn high. The waistcoat is purposely left open over the stomach for ventilation and a place to rest the hand (or even warm it!); sometimes the cravat is pulled through this opening. His hose are of dark gray wool and are worn with black shoes with a large tongue flap and silver buckle. Hannah's corset (see Plate 6) now has the sleeves tied in place and the ribbons tucked and hidden. A "busk," a wedge-shaped piece of wood covered with cloth, has been slipped in the bodice front to hide the corset lacings. The skirt is tied on around the waist; tabs on the bottom of the corset help to stabilize it. The lace at the sleeves and neck are part of her chemise—the chemise neck is shaped by a drawstring to conform with the shape of the corset, and the edging is carefully arranged.

In Plates 34–36, the family has separated after the Revolution. Samuel has entered politics and become a judge, and the younger couple is moving to the West to establish a land claim. Few clothes but the ones they wore were taken, and those had to be practical and durable.

Plate 34. Sarah wears a simple dress with fitted sleeves, and a pinafore with a large pocket for carrying any herbs and berries she might pick. Her stole is a keepsake quilt she made from scraps of material given to her by friends and relations from home. Benjamin wears his farmer outfit with the addition of full-length Native American leggings and moccasins. The younger children are dressed in simple homespun attire. Ruth carries a precious scarf given to her by her grandmother. Thomas carries a small bow and arrow.

Plate 35. Prudence wears a woolen cape for protection from the elements. Her corset is cut low (a practical style for nursing babies) and is filled out with her chemise. She wears a narrow apron and sturdy walking shoes. For traveling, John adopts the Native American-inspired frontier attire worn by hunters and trappers. His garments are of soft leather and he wears moccasins and leggings. His fur hat is decorated with feathers.

Plate 36. Samuel wears a judicial robe similar to those worn in England and France by clerics and officials. His white ceremonial wig resembles wigs still worn today in the English courts. Hannah's dress is of lavender taffeta and the skirt is decorated with ruching of the same fabric; the sleeves are caught with pink velvet garters that are studded with pearls. She wears a matching pink velvet cape caught over one shoulder and pinned to the other.

Note: The abbreviations on the clothing tabs indicate for which person (or group) the garment is intended: BE for Benjamin, RT for Ruth and Thomas, SR for Sarah, PR for Prudence, JN for John, SM for Samuel, and HA for Hannah.

CLOTHING OF THE FEDERAL PERIOD
(**NOTE:** The dolls are on Plates 7 to 9; Their costumes are on Plates 37 to 48)

By the early 1800s, the young United States was an exploding society, both politically and socially. Like the country, the fashions of the early 1800s were in transition. Because most Americans had to make their own clothing, garments were cared for to last many years, and fashions in the new land changed slowly by today's standards. New styles originated in Europe, usually in Paris or London, and were copied from prints or, occasionally, originals that were brought by tourists or visitors. Many of the European Empire or Regency styles were given a distinct American flavor in translation, which is called "Federal."

John and his wife, Prudence, had migrated to the West, but shortly after their arrival, Prudence died in childbirth. John married Maria Lucretia ("Mary Lou") Gripon, who had also been widowed in her family's trek to the new territory. In 1810, John and Mary Lou decided to move back to his family's farm in the East. With them they took Mary Lou's son, Walter, and his wife, Patricia, with their young children, Stan,

Sharon, and Tom, and John's two youngest children, Hal and Kathy, now teenagers. John and Mary Lou's older children remained in the territory.

Plate 7. Mary Lou wears a long English dimity corset laced in back. It is stiffened by parallel rows of stitching. Under her corset she wears a soft chemise. John wears a shirt whose tail is tucked into his long drawers, which have a front flap.

Plate 8. Walter wears a soft shirt that ties at the neck and is gathered for fullness. His long, knitted wool underwear has a side flap opening. The undervest is of flannel, a fabric popular for men's and women's winter undergarments because, for its weight, it was warmer than any other material. Patricia wears a chemise with a damask "zona," or corselet, which is single-laced in front and has a muslin-covered buckram busk slipped under the lacings to prevent cutting or chafing. The zona has shoulder straps that cross in the back for support.

Plate 9. Hal wears two-piece woolen underwear. Undershirts, a fairly new fad generally adopted by the younger men, were the forerunners of the "union suit." His long, knitted underpants have a side flap and are double-buttoned at the waistband. Kathy wears a chemise under a gathered-satin "bandette" with shoulder straps of elastic-knitted webbing that cross in the back. Stan wears a scoop-necked cotton camisole top, buttoning at the shoulders, which is tucked into pantaloons fitted at the waist by a drawstring. Pantaloons, a new fashion, were a style of the French Revolution. Sharon wears a simple chemise of soft handkerchief linen gathered onto a rolled neckband. Little boys like Tom wore dresses, often until the age of four or five.

Plates 37–39 show the family of the Federal period dressed for daily work.

Plate 37. Since most of the family's clothing was made at home, Mary Lou has become an expert needleworker. Mary Lou is wearing a new dress she has just made (about 1820). It has a slightly lowered waistline and full sleeves, which are gathered on the top of the shoulder and fall loosely to the elbow, where they become more fitted. The sleeves are long enough to cover most of the hand. The skirt has a new fullness not generally seen during the first two decades of the century. The dress is topped by a detachable three-tiered collar of light cotton, the bottom two tiers having embroidery of white silk thread. John's fur-trimmed deerskin hunting coat has no lapels and has a slim, cutaway look. He wears a shirt and a wool vest. His trousers, of soft leather, probably date from his frontier days. His hat is flat and wide-brimmed.

Plate 38. Walter wears a knitted undershirt with a neckerchief. His trousers are of blue denim. His boots are double-laced, an innovation. His large-crowned, wide-brimmed hat was often worn plain, but he has creased it, as did many men of the time. Patricia wears a full-sleeved chemise of muslin under an older dress that once had detachable sleeves and has now been demoted to a housedress. Over the dress she wears a cotton work apron that ties in the back. She wears a little turban bonnet which has a sewn-in crown and ribbon decoration.

Plate 39. Hal wears a work shirt with the collar buttoned up. The shirt opens only partway down the front. He also wears the newly invented suspenders (belt loops and belts did not appear until the twentieth century),

which workingmen very quickly took up. The high-waisted, rather loose trousers are tucked into the English riding boots, favored by farmers, lumbermen, and miners, which have lined tops with the bootstraps showing. Kathy is wearing a popular, high-waisted, checked-gingham dress with a ruffle at the hem. Her muslin apron has a wide neck and large armholes, leaving rather narrow shoulder straps. Its long, narrow ties, attached at the back, are wrapped around to tie at the front, creating a high waist like the dress. She wears high-topped, pointed, laced shoes of the new patent leather. On her head she wears a cotton cloth, tied bandanna fashion. Stan is wearing a variation of Hal's costume, the only differences being in his uncreased hat and boots worn under the pants legs. Sharon wears the same style dress as her sister Kathy, but the unbelted apron has pockets. Tom wears a chemise covered by a cotton apron and one of his sister's old, starched, brimmed cotton bonnets to protect him from the sun.

Plates 40–45 show the family in dressier attire.

Plate 40. On market day Mary Lou dons her best bonnet, made of sheer linen with ribbon loops around the face and descending onto side lappets that end in a generous bow under the chin. She also wears her best hand-made tatted-lace collar. Her velvet dress is of the newer style, with a slightly lowered waistband that buttons at the front. Although the skirt is gathered at the waist, most of the fullness occurs at the back and sides of the garment, giving a straight-fronted appearance. The full-topped sleeves feature a tie-band at the wrist that allows the length of the sleeve to be adjusted. John is wearing an older-style suit (ca. 1801) featuring a cutaway coat with a fold-back lapel, high collar, and cuffs at the sleeves that fold down over part of the hands. The coat fits snugly through the body, shoulders, and sleeves, a style that had completely changed by 1820. His short, straight-cut vest is of striped silk; an over-the-chin silk cravat is wrapped around his neck twice, ending in a tied knot. The top hat, with a rather wide brim and flared crown, is soft, in contrast to the stiff-crowned hats of a few years later. He wears the older-style knee breeches and stockings and cloth slippers with a silver buckle.

Plate 41. For market day, Walter wears a suit similar to that of his stepfather, the principal difference being its more conservative black woolen fabric. The coat features the "claw hammer" tails, as did John's. His hat, of a later vintage, is the harder-crowned topper. Although the suit jackets of the day could be buttoned, they were usually worn open, except in the coldest weather. Patricia wears a day dress, dating from around 1804. It is made of white-on-white embroidered cotton and has a spencer of flowered chintz. Her bonnet has a very narrow brim and pleated poufs in the crown.

Plate 42. Hal has joined the Marines and is home on leave. He wears the uniform that was seen at the shores of Tripoli (1804) as well as in the War of 1812. The American military uniforms of this period were similar to those of the French, with cutaway coats so curved back that they could scarcely be seen from the front. The lapels were purely decorative; they could no longer be buttoned, the jacket being fastened across the chest by two hooks. Kathy wears a modified Empire gown. The neckline is quite low and wide with a narrow sheer collar or edging. The sleeves, though puffed, do not stand up at the shoulders and are flared so that all of the fullness is at their lowest point. The skirt of the dress, though full, is of such a soft fabric that it falls straight. Her bonnet and her reticule are of satin. She carries a shawl that Hal brought her from North Africa. She wears satin slippers. Stan is dressed in a jacket and pantaloons. The tail of the jacket is rounded so that it becomes a cutaway. He has a plain vest over a low, round-necked blouse. His kerchief is tucked into the neck of the shirt and the vest. His slippers are of felt. Sharon's dress has a wide, low neck and fitted sleeves, both of which are edged with a band of satin ribbon and lace edging. The dress is of a soft print cotton with a wide sash that has been folded to be narrower. Tom wears a soft cotton dress with a kerchief tucked into the neckline.

Plate 43. For cold weather, Mary Lou wears a velvet coat trimmed in lapin [rabbit]. Her matching bonnet has a satin ribbon and bow. This style of coat, called a "redingote," remained fashionable for a number of years, appearing in several lengths. Although more sensible for cold-weather wear, redingotes did not replace the stole and shawl, which remained the most popular form of winter outerwear for women through the 1850s. Mary Lou's coat has a fitted bodice with a skirt that flares slightly in front and, by means of pleats, is quite full in back. The sleeves are full at the top and fit closely the lower arm and upper part of the hands. The cape comes to the waistline and has a stand-up collar. It is fastened down the front with self buttons held by braided loops. The bonnet is of the coal-scuttle variety, the chin ribbon holding the brim quite close to the face. John wears a woolen Garrick coat, named after the English actor, David Garrick. Sometimes called a coachman's coat, it featured one to three short capes over the shoulders. The tail of the coat is flared to allow freedom in mounting and dismounting a horse. The closures are double-buttoned flaps. He wears Hessian boots and a winter hat with a small brim and a deep, somewhat conical, crown of felt with a silken cord.

Plate 44. Walter's heavy woolen winter coat has a tight waist with a full skirt. The sleeves are gathered at the shoulder, giving them a fullness at the top, tapering to become fitted from the elbow down to the long cuff, which is folded back. The double-breasted closure becomes a notched collar when the coat is worn open. He wears English riding boots and a felt top hat. Patricia is dressed in a satin sacque over which she wears a crocheted woolen stole or shawl. A soft white kerchief is tucked into the neckline of the dress and flipped over the shawl. She also wears full-length kid gloves and a bonnet called a "jockey's hat," styled after the jockeys' hats worn in Paris.

Plate 45. Hal, who has now left the Marines, is dressed in a "Polish" cape. It has one short cape around the shoulders, but could have as many as three. His suit has a short, double-breasted jacket with claw-hammer tails and features a velvet stand-up collar. He wears a silk cravat under a vest with stand-up lapels. The trousers have front slash pockets edged in brown gimp. His top hat is of beaver. Kathy's dress is of satin with an Empire waistline. For fullness, the bodice is gathered lightly both above and below the bosom. The full, clinging skirt

has a row of satin swags near the hemline. A satin belt with a silver brooch in the center sets off the waistline. The sleeves are puffed at the top with three rows of puffed satin shirring that form rolls, and cuffs made of the shirred satin rolls. Her collar is of starched lace that stands up around the back of the neckline, and she carries a shawl of white machine-made lace. What appears to be pantalettes are not; they are leggings, tied just below the knees, and worn for warmth as much as for modesty. Her satin shoes have ties around the ankle. Her bag is of satin and the rope wound around her neck is of clear crystal beads ending in silken tassels. Her hat, styled after a man's top hat, is trimmed with lace and a satin hatband and bow. Stan wears a coat similar to his father's, although it is cut shorter. His trousers are notched at the bottom and have a drop seat for convenience. His wide collar is held up by a cravat. He wears cloth slippers. Sharon is wearing an Empire-line coat with an ermine collar. The opening of the coat is a modified cutaway and the trim is appliquéd bands of satin ribbon. Her dress has an eyelet flounce at the hem, under which she wears pantalettes. The dress has a Dolly Madison ruff or "betsy" for a collar. Her bonnet, of the same velvet as the coat, is molded over a buckram frame and is trimmed in velvet ribbon. Tom wears a tam and coat-dress of plaid wool trimmed with velvet. Under it he wears a shirt, pantalettes, and slippers and stockings.

Plates 46–48 show the family dressed for Kathy's wedding.

Plate 46. Mary Lou wears a satin Empire gown with an overdress of lace-edged net, crossing at the bosom to soften the neckline. The short, puffed sleeves have a net ruffle. Her turban, of watered satin, sports an ostrich plume. The folds of the turban are caught in front by a large pearl clip. She wears a long, paisley stole of natural lightweight wool. She has long, kid gloves and is carrying a satin fan edged with marabou. John has chosen to wear a velvet jacket with claw-hammer tails and brass buttons. The breeches are a little old-fashioned, but they are still appropriate for a man of his years.

Plate 47. Walter's velvet jacket is of the same general styling as his stepfather's. His wool trousers are worn tucked into his leather Hessian boots, and the trousers button from the knee down to give a snugger fit. His hat is of beaver. The square-cut vest is of striped satin and he wears two watch fobs of striped silk. Patricia wears her best formal gown of watered silk taffeta in the Empire style. The neckline is quite low and the small, dainty sleeves stop at the same level as the neckline. The sleeve and the neckline are bound in rolled satin ribbon. The bottom of the skirt is decorated with four flounces of lace topped by a row of tiny silk ribbon florettes. Her slippers, fan, and bag are of satin and she wears a paisley stole. Her necklace is a double strand of pearls with a large rose quartz; her rose quartz earrings match.

Plate 48. Hal, the best man at Kathy's wedding, is wearing a new outfit that he had sent from Europe, featuring lower, square-cut lapels and a single-breasted closure with decorative buttons that gives a double-breasted V-shaped effect. The jacket also has the newer swallowtails that are fuller at the hip, giving a rounded effect. The tails are also longer, dropping to knee level. A frill, rather than a cravat, is worn at the neck. His trousers are of lightweight shadow-striped wool and he wears spats over his patent-leather slippers. Brad wears his officer's uniform. Kathy's dress shows the trend of the 1830s toward the lower waistline and the more Romantic full skirt. The sleeves are becoming larger and more puffed out. Her satin gown is trimmed with embroidered satin ribbon in a rose-and-leaf design. The cameo neckline leaves her shoulders bare, and the full skirt ends in a double ruffle with scalloped edges. Her headdress is of silk roses with a tulle veil. She carries a bouquet of roses, white lilac, and baby's breath. Stan, the ring bearer, is wearing a velvet suit with pantaloons and jacket buttoned together, giving a one-piece effect. The sleeveless blouse has a wide collar that extends to the shoulderline.

Sharon wears a dress of watered-taffeta, the same fabric as her mother's. It has low shoulders with a sheer-fabric shawl collar. The sleeves are puffed and the dress has a wide set-in waistband. Under the dress she wears pantalettes. Her hat is in the mobcap style with lace edging on the ruffle. Tom wears a collarless velvet jacket over a white baby's dress with a large collar.

Note: The abbreviations on the clothing tabs indicate for which person (or group) the garment is intended: ML for Mary Lou, JN for John, WA for Walter, PT for Patricia, SST for the group Stan, Sharon, and Tom, HL for Hal, and KA for Kathy.

CLOTHING OF THE CIVIL WAR PERIOD
(NOTE: The dolls are on Plates 10 to 12; Their costumes are on Plates 49 to 60)

The Civil War years (1861–1865) saw little change in fashion: it was a time for altering, mending, and making do with clothes one already had. Most clothing styles shown here, therefore, actually date from the decade before the war.

During the 1850s some typical American styles were developing in "folk" or work clothes, such as buckskins, sunbonnets, cowboy outfits, denim, double-breasted or "cavalry" shirts, and the scandalous Amelia Jenks Bloomer's "bloomers." In addition, the sewing machine was finding its way into many American homes as well as into the factory, creating a new clothing industry as the first attempts were made to mass-produce fashion. The first machine-made shoes appeared at this time. The growing industrial momentum brought affordable fashion to everyone.

"The Age of the Crinoline" is an apt name for this fashion era, since the crinoline, or hoopskirt, dominated women's silhouettes. The stiffened horsehair petticoat of the earlier Romantic era had, by the 1850s, become a wire cage for holding out the skirt. At the height of the hoopskirt period, skirts measured up to six feet across, although the average was nearer four feet. Dresses were usually made in two parts, the skirt and the bodice.

As the Industrial Revolution overtook America, successful businessmen sought the loftier, more distinguished appearance of statesmen. The image of the lawyer-statesman seen in the Mathew Brady photographs of Abraham Lincoln embodied an ideal; the business uniform of the day became the sober black suit, white linen, tall silk hat, black scarf tie, and boots or gaiters. As for children's clothes, they were simply smaller versions of the adult modes.

The paper dolls on Plates 10–12 portray three generations of an American family of the Civil War era. Their clothes show what would have been considered appropriate costumes in several different situations.

Grandmother Ruth, now 75, was the younger daughter of John and Prudence in the Colonial Period Paper Dolls. Grandfather Gregory, a successful businessman, and a gentleman farmer, has reached the age of 80. Their son, Theodore, is in business with his father. Theodore and Julia, his wife, have four children of their own: Christine, 16 years old; Richard, 9; Kenneth, 7; and Annie, age 5. Tom, a young man of 18 from a neighboring family, is Christine's fiancé.

Plate 10. Gregory wears knitted red woolen undershirt and drawers, both with knitted cuffs. The drawers are held by thin, lightweight suspenders that button on. His slippers have carpet-fabric tops and felt soles. Ruth wears a rather old-fashioned "Swiss petticoat" and short chemise of 1840s vintage. This type of petticoat, the forerunner of the hooped crinoline, has parallel rows of stitching around the bottom to give it the stiffness required to hold out the full skirts. She is probably wearing several other similar petticoats under this one to give even more fullness and body. She carries a sewing case made of the same type of carpet fabric as Gregory's slippers. Her ribboned, ballet-style slippers are also a little out of fashion but still popular with the older generation. Gregory has broad side-whiskers, an absolute must for any adult male in this era. (Beards and moustaches were also seen quite frequently.) Had he enough hair, it would probably have a center part. Women's hairstyles were almost always parted in the center and often separated into flattened strands or plaits drawn down over the cheeks and then looped back up over the ears into a knot or bun. If curly, the hair was often pulled to the sides from the center part into bunches of frizzed curls. For more formal occasions the hair was rolled onto rags to set overnight, then combed into long bunches of corkscrew curls (see Plate 12). By the outbreak of the war, these side curls were beginning to disappear from fashion as simpler hair treatments came into favor (see Plates 53 and 60).

Plate 11. Julia is wearing a crinoline "pouf" with steel hoops and ribbon ties. Under the crinoline she wears a plain petticoat over a back-laced whalebone corset with reinforced stitching in the front and detachable sleevelets. Theodore wears a gray knitted wool "union suit" (so called not for the Union, as opposed to the Confederacy, but for its union of top and bottom in a single one-piece garment). Over the union suit he wears a red flannel underwaistcoat. His slippers are of red plush.

Plate 12. Christine wears steel hoops held by tapes over a muslin petticoat. Her corset is back-laced, reinforced in front and at the sides with whalebone stays. She is also wearing ankle-length pantalets. Richard is wearing a muslin, one-piece bodice and drawers with a drawstring waist and ties at the knees. Kenneth wears a muslin undershirt and separate short drawers. The waist is fitted by means of ties at the side and back. Annie wears a simple muslin chemise over pantalets. The neck and sleeves of the chemise are trimmed in pale yellow embroidered ribbon. Tom wears a knit undershirt and drawers, both made of silkaline, a newly developed cotton-and-silk blend used for underwear. The cuffs are knitted wool; the waistband of the drawers is muslin and can be adjusted with side tapes.

The first set of costumes (Plates 49–51) dresses the family in work clothes.

Plate 49. Gregory is wearing a gray wool shirt in the cavalry style, with a double-breasted front closure for warmth. His pants are not belted but held by suspenders that button at the waist. He has a broad-brimmed hat with a rounded crown. Ruth is wearing a deep green, cotton sateen dress; bands of satin ribbon have been stitched in place with white silk thread to form a pattern. The collar is white muslin with embroidered edging.

Plate 50. Julia's housedress is of yellow, red, and tan plaid gingham. The bodice is canvas-lined for extra strength and warmth. This dress was often worn hoopless when doing heavier chores or working in the garden. She wears an apron; nearly every woman of the era wore an apron at some time during the day, for cooking, sewing, cleaning, or gardening, and there was a different size apron for almost every chore. Theodore wears a blue denim pullover work shirt (the coat shirt, which buttons all the way down the front, was a later development) with cotton work pants. He wears a blue sash instead of a belt. His knee-high boots, the most common footwear East or West at this time, are for both work and dress occasions. He wears a soft felt hat with a medium brim and moderate crown.

Plate 51. Christine wears a pink-and-brown, over-sized-check gingham dress with leg-o'-mutton puffed sleeves. The apron of dark brown canvas has the same neckline as the dress but is worn lower, off the shoulder. The apron buttons to the waist in the back and is then open to the skirt. At the wrists, satin ribbons fastened with a brooch hold her sleeves tightly. Richard wears a red, wool, pullover work shirt with gray cotton work pants held up by suspenders; he wears high-topped shoes. Kenneth wears a similar work shirt in blue denim, also with gray cotton trousers. Annie wears a red-and-gray checkered dress styled like her sister's and a red apron with scalloped edges. She wears white pantalets fitted at the ankle and red patent-leather shoes. Tom is dressed for hunting and trapping in a Native American-style buckskin coat with long fringes. Besides being decorative, fringes had practical purposes: they drained off rain from the body of the coat and were a ready source of binding thongs. Tom wears a blue denim pullover shirt, brown wool trousers, and, instead of a belt, a Native American-style sash. He wears high-topped natural-leather boots and a broad-brimmed, low-crowned felt hat, and carries a rifle.

The second group of costumes (Plates 52–54) shows the family in day wear.

Plate 52. Gregory is wearing a frock coat of black wool, matching trousers, and a brocaded satin vest. His cravat is starched so that it stands out. Top hat and boots complete his outfit. Ruth wears a wine-colored velvet dress based on a drawing of a gown, designed by the Englishman Charles Frederick Worth, that she found in a ladies' magazine. Such a dress with matching jacket eventually developed into the tailored suit of the twentieth century. This early form of the suit featured a peplum skirt that dipped in the back, presaging the bustle. The shoulders were accented with rolls of padded material or "wings." The skirt to this suit-dress was generally longer in back, giving a train effect. Contrasting braid decorates the closure of the jacket and the edge of the skirt. Her hat is a flat, derby-like affair with ostrich plumes, rather like the riding hat Worth designed for Empress Eugénie of France. She carries a silk parasol and an ivory-handled fan.

Plate 53. Julia's "at home" dress is inspired by the Amelia Jenks Bloomer dress of 1850. The full sleeves split in front to show full, soft undersleeves. (Sometimes these sleeves were detachable, other times part of a full blouse worn underneath the garment; the white collar was also either detachable or part of a full blouse.) The collar was always caught at the throat with a brooch. The stiffly boned bodice and the weighty skirt were separate. Grosgrain ribbon makes the trim and the wide poufed sashes that decorate the skirt. Aniline dyes had recently been invented and brilliant colors—violets, magentas, fuchsias—were becoming popular. Theodore wears a brown wool frock coat, cut rather loosely; fawn-color trousers; and a brown silk, brocaded waistcoat. He has a tucked shirt with a pre-tied tie and detachable collar. (Cuffs were also now detachable; travelers could freshen their collars and cuffs without having to change shirts.)

Plate 54. Christine's summer dress is of muslin printed in a paisley pattern of coral and white. The jacket is worn over a handkerchief linen blouse. The fingertip-length jacket is deceptive—the flounce just below the waistline makes the jacket appear shorter than it is. The skirt is in three tiers. Richard wears his new bicycling outfit; as a development in fashion design, sportswear was still a novel concept, destined to father a new industry. His sports suit is checkered wool in ocher tones, but such suits were also made in corduroy, tweed, or linen for summer, and worn for other outdoor activities, such as hiking, fishing, and sport shooting. The coat has a cutaway front skirt for freedom of movement. It features plenty of flapped pockets; often, a shoulder strap and pouch were added to carry large items required for one's sport. Buff-color gaiters or leggings are worn over the trousers and over high-topped lace-up shoes. The matching visored cap has flaps turned up inside which can also be worn down to protect the ears. He wears a white shirt with turned-down collar points and a black bow tie. Kenneth's plaid collarless shirt, full-cut with puffed sleeves, somewhat like a short tunic, is worn tucked into knee pants with a buttoned waistband. He wears high-topped laced shoes and long white stockings. Annie's dress of blue gingham is trimmed with pleated white lawn and worn with a white sash, white stockings, and black high-topped shoes. Tom's summer suit of tan cotton broadcloth is worn with a black satin, striped silk waistcoat. His wide-brimmed hat has a flat crown, and he wears brown high-topped shoes.

In Plates 55–57 the members of the family are dressed for winter.

Plate 55. Gregory's double-breasted wool hammertail